Life's *Abundant* Treasure Chest

By William Borum, Jr.

Preface

In 1991, the World of Poetry, over 1.7 million poets strong (worldwide) presented William an award merit certificate for the poem "A Child's Thoughts". He has received a Golden Poet trophy for the poem "Zeal Where Art Thou" (Changed to 'Lamentation'), and is listed as one of the best new poets of 1988 by the American Poetry Association.

William Borum, affectionately known to his friends as 'Zeke', decided one day, during a spell of illness to write about his life in poetry, prose, and short stories. He was not sure he could write another poem or anything after his first poem, but through perseverance and inspiration, he began writing poem after poem. Then he fell into a dry spell, for lack of a better word, 'the mind went blank'. he would began again. Anyone going through similar struggles and need understanding of how to cope when life takes a turn against you, and If you are determined to make a success after a two year layoff. These writings are intended to help someone like himself who did not live a good family life as a child. Now a mature man in his seventies he looks back remembering his roots and thanking God that the experience made him a better person. He is now happily married and has struggled and sacrificed his life to the Lord Jesus Christ. He is now a leader in the Church of God In Christ. All of his writings point back to his childhood which he has never regretted. These writings are geared to help you with problems in your life.

Table of CONTENT

Life's *Abundant* Treasure Chest

The Superior Race

First White brother to the second White brother..

"Look here man, the company bought a new computer. It was extremely difficult to understand; but with much perseverance, I finally understand the concept. It took me about a month to comprehend its many functions."

First Black brother to the second Black brother: "Look here man the company bought a new computer. It was extremely difficult to understand, but with much perseverance, I finally understand the concept. It took me about a month to comprehend its many functions."
First Black brother to the first White brother: "Hey man I finally learned how to use the new computer, man it was not easy. Was it difficult for you?"
First White brother to the first Black brother: "No man, piece a cake!"   ***

2

Mommy, ..
Daddy's Gone

Beneath the loft
Sitting on a staircase bench,
Blanket covered, huddled
together, sat all six of us-
Swaying side to side,
chanting: "Mommy... Mommy...
Mommy-"
Words,...forsaken, ...minds
quietly milling... all in one accord.
The pantry is empty... where
are you Mommy?"

The rain spotted our beds last night; we slept on the plank covered beams. Through the riddled dome, the moon and the stars appeared as a silken glow... as the water
welded the cracks. The thoughts then burst into the atmosphere, as voices continue, ... now verbally expressed — Chanting: "Mommy... Mommy... Where are you mommy?"

4

Dad displayed a host of the
presidents last night; but not one
of them escaped from his hand
to ours. He partied every night
this week-- all night,
while strange men and women
roamed the house.
They tried to give us money, but
we would not take it.
One woman with tears in her
eyes begged us to take the
money, but we would not take it.
Chanting: "Mommy...Mommy,
where have you gone?"

5

Some nights, men and women together, creaked the bed. Springs-- they mourn and groan- and tell each other pleasant things; while we listen from our bedroom door.

They cry loud, then silence, the snoring, the walking, the cursing, and departing, all through the night.

Chanting:

"Mommy...Mommy...Mommy" then the only soprano breaks into tears, shouting "daddy's gone now. Mommy, please come back home."

The Attitudes
(7th Grade Students)

"Why do we have all these classes? We go back and forth all day long that's dumb. This school is like a prison, you can't talk in the classroom. We have important things to tell our friends.

Why do we have to follow all these dumb rules?

The teacher is always interrupting our conversations in class,

but they tell us not to interrupt
them when they are conversing
with an adult. That's not fair!

When we talk out and they want
to give us detention, but they
talk out whenever they want to,
that's not fair!"
"They expect me to do all my
homework when I am tired.
When we have a test I don't see
why once in a while the teacher
couldn't give us some answers.
Why can't we have fun in the
classroom when we are here all
day.

They don't respect us, why
should I respect them?
Why does the school continue
to make all of these dumb rules?
I am not doing it."

Dad's Day
Happy Father's Day Dad!

A true love at all times. He plans to support his family. No job is too hard or too long. When need presents her calling card, he stands ready to protect his family at the slightest provocation.

He prays for the Lord's divine direction in every decision concerning the emotional, financial, intellectual and social stability of his charge.

He prays that his family will take heed to the Word of God, and live thereby. He expresses his love in words and in deeds. His discipline is not given through anger or strife, but through love, gentleness and understanding. He's patient, trustworthy and easily taken advantage of by his family. His son claims "no one can lick my dad."

His daughter knows she is his little princess. His wife feels secure in is his love and providing.

Deliverance Shall Come

He was fourteen, strong and
athletic,
Captain of the Black Panthers
basketball team.
Of the poor, he was poorer. He
felt shame,
but wore it like a badge of
courage.

Those who thought they knew
him considered him very self
sufficient.
Here he hid his insecurity.

The problem between his mom
and dad immaculate Went back
to his childhood.
His dad was a gambler, smooth
talker .popular with the ladies -
handsome, dresser.

His mom prettier than most, shy,
innocent, good moral upbringing.
His dad a heavy drinker, victim
of his past.

Over the years, his mom became
victim of his physical abuse.
Once her face was disfigured
almost beyond recognition.

His dad was away from home
weeks at a time.

Those were the peaceful days.

His mom taught them never to
speak against their father.

Bill was the oldest.

The burden of his mom's
physical abuse hung heavier on
his shoulders than any of his
brothers.

One Saturday morning, June
1948, his dad came home after a
drinking spree and began
beating his mom. She screamed
and called out her oldest son's
name. From the adjoining room

Bill leaped and pinned his dad against the wall holding him while screaming, "Leave my mother alone!" He couldn't hit his father, he just held him there until he felt he had made his point. He released him, ran, and jumped down a twelve step staircase. His dad threw a gallon jug after him.

He didn't have to leave his home until he was twenty-one. Not one incident of physical abuse occurred from that day forward. "Thank God" he reminisces, "I never struck my father."

15

Fifth Grade

(Typical classroom scene 1999)

The fog horn
bellows
The hallways fill.
The class enters
A confusion of noise ensues.
A raging sea beating upon the
rocks, is a quiet place to be.
Distress calls back and forth
An established mode of
communication.
A slamming door follows,
each grand entry.
Heavy books forcibly slap the
desk and the floors.

An explosion of chatter
(common)
"Teacher can we use the
computer?"
On your mark, get set, go
The race is on...
"Please, be quiet!"
A muffled passionate plea
ignored,
Perhaps not heard
"Please be quiet!"
A little louder this time.
"This is your last warning -
alright
Travis, you got your detention"

Twenty minutes later:
"Start working on your
homework"
Balls of paper make a cameo
appearance (in flight) across the
classroom to its intended
destination.
The teacher expounds her
lesson, interrupting the children's
conversation.
The fog horn bellows again.
Time to go --
Papers cover the floor like the
fourth of July cleanup on New
York City streets.

A race to the door is protocol
forming a proper line before
leaving.

The classroom is near
impossible.
Another class enters to
rehearse the same rules.
The scene rehearsed across the
nation,
Prayer was legally taken out of
the schools. The good was
taken out, the evil rejoiced.
The Christians stood by and
allowed this to happen.
The parents stood by and
allowed this to happen.

The devil is the author of
confusion --Have you checked
out school classrooms lately.

Short Arm of the Law

The phone rings
A calm voice
announces --
"the bulls are coming." Click!
Dad's calm turns to panic. He
frantically
rummages the clothes closets,
the dresser drawers. His
streamlined carrying case with a
bunch of paper in hand.., he runs
out the front door.   The car
motor turns over -- He drives
speedily away. Upon his return
he appears more reserved.

The phone rings again. --false
alarm! ok. Click.

Outside the door a motorcycle
approaches a highly respected
uniformed cop walks through the
front door.

"Hey Buddy, take care of this"
He handed dad a slip, but no
money. "Take care of this
Buddy".

"Okay" my dad replied.
Protection money I suspect. My
father's profession --banker in
the numbers game.

Fearful Nights

The child awakened downstairs
in this broken little house.
The familiar voice of his mom
and dad raised in anger had
invaded his sleep.
He cringed in fear, "don't let it
get any louder," he thought to
himself, ..but it did.

Please Lord, don't let the rumble
come. ... it came. Tears began to
moisten his frightened face. I
can't do anything. he despaired.

His thoughts frantically
searching for direction. If I cry
out, maybe they'll stop.
"Daddy, please don't hurt
mommy!"
His voice breaking the silence
from the
upstairs bedroom -- but to no
avail.
He shook his brother who lay
quiet beside him, sharing his
anguish, he cried out---
"They're fighting again. "
" Buddy please don't hit me
again!" their mother screamed --
every scream was like a knife
piercing their fragile bodies.

24

The home shook... pots, pans,
dishes fell ...crashing to the floor.
Between their mother's constant
pleas,
"Please don't hit me!"
The bed covers offered their
only refuge. His prayers finally
answered -- The silence came
as the whimpering subsided.

Days of Imagination and Common Sense

Gone with the wind, and the weather we suppose,
Are those days when oatmeal, wheaties, and corn flakes,
Tasted like the ice cream, coke and candy of today,
Milk was supreme, soda pop had not yet made its début at our house. The days were not long enough for us. Every day held its own adventure and we were poor, but we didn't own it.

Mom, pop, my brothers, and sisters filled my world of expectation. We took in a little dog, which we named Fluffy. He was my best friend. Life to us kids was exciting! and challenging. If we needed or wanted a bicycle, we found parts in the better economic neighborhood's sidewalk trash . We made scooters using skate wheels, two in the front, and two in the back, nailed to a flat board (kin to today's skateboard) added a handle to its upright post, painted it and rode all day long

Our wagons were made from baby carriage wheels we attached them to two short boards; a long plank, a wooden box at one end; a rope attached to the steering board at the other end and rode the streets all

day long. In the winter, we found wooden barrel staves and attached them to a box and went sleigh riding on those type of barrel staves, waxed the bottom , put straps in the middle of them to secure our feet, ...found a steep hill and skied all day.

We were the thinkers and the builders. We thought that the expression "being bored" was drilling a hole into a piece of wood.

In those days, none of our communities had a TV. "What was that?" we had radios, we listened to the Lone Ranger, the Shadow, Fibber McKee, and Molly and Flash Gordon, to name a few. Our imaginations supplied the sight as we listened to the radio audibly.

Dope was someone who we thought acted or was stupid. Gay was a word used to express a joyous lively person. The movies had made their appearance but it was years before many of us were able to afford them. - Boys an girls, from the beginning were at times naughty, ... so be it.

Church was our main source of entertainment and social activity, but the butt of many jokes.

In those days, negroes as whole were told that our main employment in life would be mediocre. "He who laughs last laughs best".

———————————————

Forgiven

I once knew a man who didn't
have time for his wife,
He was gambling man, he didn't
have time for his children
He was a popular man, his time
belonged to his following.
He wore spats, dapper Dan
suits and tap dance shoes.
He protected his friends from
his family,
He fathered a large family but
his life belonged to his
supporting public.
Young love, innocent
unsuspecting,

32

Different upbringing, moral
differences, clashing.
You know the beauty and the
beast syndrome.
Liquor and fast living compliment
each other.
But is acid to a marriage—
Divorce ensued.
His children kept in touch
After all he was dad.

When age slowed him down, he
mellowed.
Sickness and affliction claimed
his vibrant body,

Except for one, (exactly like him)
his children grew closer to him.
His new wife welcomed the
estranged family to visit in their
old home.
On his death bed, he asked his
ex-wife to forgive him—— then
cried like a baby, ... she forgave
him.

———————————————

Alone Again

Her seasoned years were upon
her
Hanging loosely like drapery,
resting upon her shoulders. Her
hair streaked in black and gray.
Misty eyed... she bowed her
head remembering once again
her past.
After many years of broken
promises, happiness had eluded
her grasp.
Finally, upon that bleak horizon
a ray of sunshine appears,

She consented to a marriage proposal before her fruitful years were abandoned.

She told anyone who would listen, "my husband is a good man" The old house built by inexperienced hands, was worse for wear, Needing repair but happiness would not elude her again.

This was her old home. I'll make do, she reasoned, I'm thankful for what God has provided. She was proud of her two boys.

She taught them to fear God.
Time stood still for her from any
activities outside their home for
three years.

Primetime unencumbered to raise
her two boys. At the appointed
time her husband passed on
leaving her with what little he had
provided.

Her children soon moved out to
seek their own God given
destiny. She thought the ghost
of the past had abandoned her.

But the lonely nights and the empty house brought them back as vivid as every incident had occurred. *Alone again* ... uncertain of the future. She gave herself to prayer On any given day, (around noon), if you listen very intently, you will hear the anguished cry of a lonely widow, ..calling on her God. (*Alone again, ..naturally.*)

Food for Thought

When we are born our direction or road we choose is pre decided predicated upon the environment that embrace us. How do we escape our environment when we don't know of any reason to escape? Or, how do we know to accept a fate or direction that will be a positive force in our lives?

Much too often we don't We respond or react according to what we see and to the dictates of all our senses.

We strongly react to the feelings that lie deep within us, although many times we do not understand them.

Before we are able to know, accept or correct our direction, we have been programmed to think as we have been taught, or led to believe,

the independent thinker can be a curse or a God sent depending on what course of life he chooses to follow.

The beginning of knowledge and wisdom is God.

Who knows each individual better, in fact, than the individual knows themselves. How then do we find our true direction without a close relationship with God... or at the very least, ask for his direction which would, in itself, tend to bring us closer to his divine will. All the issues of life are found in the scriptures. The road that leads to good health, prosperity and fulfilling success... has already been paved. Read your Bible --Ask God why he sent you here?

Ironic

Two sisters birthed from the same womb, one is older.

The younger more attractive to many.

The same opportunities were provided. Both embraced their mothers love but jealousy and covetousness is a cruel task master. Throughout their lives the younger will try to appease the older. Both married, both raised large families, but the older sister has an affair with the younger sister's husband.

Rivalry between sisters spun a thread of jealousy between the innocent first cousins.

The silent question. Who has the better children?

This secretly discussed behind closed doors. Subtly implied in open conversation at the gatherings. The older shows no religious concerns... Both are now divorced. The younger sister has another opportunity for marital bliss. Again, the older sister steals her younger sister's choice.

The younger sister finds satisfaction in dedicating her life to helping others. The older sister continues to pursue a life of selfishness. The younger sister has long expired, ... years later, the older sister lives on.

————————————

LOOK
Before You Leap

I called her last night,
Her anguished tone mellowed
when she recognized my voice.
"Hi" she replied, (I answered),
"How are you today?" "I detect
a tenseness in your voice, not
usually present". "You do", she
said, "Well, my husband and I
have just had one of our many
confrontations. I'm at the point
of leaving him."

With all the tenderness I could muster, words of experience began to flow. At this cross roads, in your twenty-five years of marriage.... "Think carefully, what you are saying, why would you leave a good man in search of a good man.

You see his faults. Do you see your own?" "He loves you.. True love doesn't come often, You say you have comfort and security now, but should you realize later you made a bad decision; loneliness and delusion will be constant reminders. Stay put, consult God... Work diligently to rebuild your marriage. It is important that you respect your marriage and your husband at all times.

Don't burn down your bridges, ... should you decide to end your marriage. Be very very sure you are mentally, socially, and financially prepared for the consequences that follow. You can't hang out with inexperienced singles and your close friends don't want you around their husbands.

The divorcees don't want any competition. After you leave the protection of your husband, you will find most men looking for one night stands. The wolves in sheep's clothing will come-a-knocking at your door for you to support them. So, where do you fit in. Please take it slow. The death of a marriage is a traumatic experience at its best."

"I will consider that," she replied

And hung up the phone.

A Widow's Psalm

Pray a little prayer for me,
My heavy heart is lonely
While thinking of my one and only.
Death claimed him when I needed him most.
Pray a little prayer for me.
He made my life exciting,
His soft embrace... so warm and inviting,
Leaves turning on the sycamore tree.
Pray a little prayer for me.

I miss him every season,
My love for him defies all reason,
Snow flakes driven like the raging sea,
Pray a little prayer for me.
Tho' in His eternal grace
I'll meet my master face to face,
Until that glorious day,
Pray a little prayer for me.

———————————

I Love Hard

When I love, I love hard
Why did God make me this way
Why doesn't anyone understand
me
True relationships seem to
elude my grasp,
Is love that hard to accept.

Someone said be careful,
Not to love man more than God,
Exhausted, disappointed,
defeated...

I turned my love toward God
He gave me love that will never
fail-
He gave me joy unspeakable,
He supplied my every need

He gave me a husband that
loved Him
He gave me children that I
taught to love Him,
He gave me a life that would
have been lost to me without
Him.

When I love , I love hard

God did not take that out of my spirit

I yet love hard, but He understands and accepts all the love I can give Him.

***

The Cricket Vessel

Behind the billowing clouds
Painting the California sky sinks
a fiery sunset
Her rays exploding across the
crimson firmament,
Like a volcanic eruption spewing
molten lava across the great
plains.

In the lowlands of South
Carolina a mother in Zion is
hanging her wash on a thin wire
line nailed between two trees
supported by two tree branches
With wish bone heads.

Typical scene, but an unusual twist.

This mother claims every night for two months a cricket chirped beneath her window.

It was the same one every night.

The burning bush attracted Moses attention.

The persistent cricket that kept his nightly vigil attracted this mother's attention.

The Lord had called her to pray a specific time each day.

She was slow to respond but from her past experiences she discerned the urging of God,

Through this small black insect,
she obeyed--
On her knees she prayed,
It was then and only then
The insects returned to the nearby field to join its fellow crickets.
There it chirped till their seasons end, I suppose.

Leaning On Thee

The Lord is my shepherd
The Lord is my guide,
When trials beset me
In him I confide,
He feels my anguish and he
knows my pain Greater is the
power
In his loving hands plenteous in
mercy enduring forever,
God of compassion I'm leaning
on thee,
Lord my provider,
Oh Lord my banner
There is no secret place hidden
from thee

Thy wondrous works, all so
awesome in nature,
Have thine own way Lord, I
worship thee,
Plenteous in Mercy, enduring
forever.
God of compassion, I'm leaning
on thee
The Lord is the captain, leading
my soul
Sojourning through this
contrary world.
He reigns supreme over all
earthly creatures,
Over all powers, all powers that
be,

Plenteous in mercy enduring forever,

God of compassion, I'm leaning on thee.

Discouraged

I had never felt this level of
depression,
Loneliness covered me like a
blanket,
Anchored by heavy chains
The house closed in on me,

I was in a coffin, a shelter of
despair,
The night darkness crept over
my house
As the closing of the lid drains
light from the inner casket.
What was I to do ? No one to
turn to.

No where to go. I was sinking to a place of no return... Out of desperation, I began to pray...
"Lord, please help me in my hour of desolation.
I raised my head to find an angel sitting in my window, dressed in purple and white.
He let me know that God said you are not alone.
On another occasion, when I felt I just couldn't take it anymore, ..another angel appeared in the likeness of my baby boy-

And he let me know that God said, you are not alone for the angels of the Lord are encamped about your house.

And yet on another occasion, when my mind again was sorely troubled, another angel appeared and took possession of my emotion.

From that point on my emotions quieted down; I sensed more boldness in my spirit.

After a few weeks, they made yet another appearance,

They assured me they were yet there for my protection.

If I should drop back in my mind,
at any given moment, I believe
they would appear again.
I thank God who promised He
would never put upon *(those that
serve him)* me, anymore than I
can bear.

Macho Man

Within the marriage vows
He claimed tradition bold,
But, equality of a female spouse
It chilled his very soul.

With his manhood challenged
Could she be as free as he?!!
Without pause came this reply,
Macho man herein lies the key
Your wife is your help meet
Everyone should understand,
She takes her place beside you.

Yes sir, macho man

The Bible says, "man love your wife, as Christ loves the Church"

He gave his life... cherish her (man's glory).

"woman obey your husband" (God's glory) Respect him.

Macho man, macho man,
Open your mind and see
Both are equal but different
And this will always be.

———————————

The Answer

Color blue my choice
Why? Is to know.
Why God chose to place that in
me.

Why? Is to know what his
thoughts were
when he preserved me
After Eden, God's garden.

Some eons ago in Adam's loins,
We laid, incubate til time brought
us to birth.

The scar, the sin
Shape of our souls

Through   centuries   of
procreation we finally came to
earth.
In time to accept our savior
Jesus Christ
Who died to save us all
Through the new birth.

––––––––––––––––––––

Have You Heard
the Good News

Have you heard the good news,
Jesus died on the cross
He suffered and died for all that
are lost.
Get your life together,
Jesus paid the price,
Surrender your ways to the
Lord Jesus Christ.

Have you heard the good news,
He raised the dead, the lame,
and the sick got up from their
bed.

Chorus:

Get in a hurry, come join this race,

If you want to see him face to face.

Kneel at the altar,

Give up the fight,

His yoke is easy and his burden is light.

Premonition
(a dream)

I saw the man of God
Sitting in his chair on a pulpit.
Fashioned by the hand of man,
But symbolic of the presence of
God.
He   sat   high   above   the
congregation,
His stature that of a servant of
God and to the people.
The saints rejoicing,
Diverted   my   attention   --
momentarily... with little notice,

he had made his way down to
the side of the pulpit,
Outside it was about dusk,
The glory of the Lord had filled

the temple--
Suddenly the crowd became a
bit uneasy,
Upon close observation, I
realized why...
The pastor's eyes looked
weaker than before,
His legs were visibly unsteady.
He looked at me and cried
aloud, "I need help!"
I awakened.

a warning from God to the Saints that an unusual sickness would come upon our Pastor,

To strengthen his faith, and encourage others to be strong in faith.

As Aaron and Joshua was to Moses, likewise we must hold up the arms of our leader. When God is our banner, we will prevail.

That Beautiful City

I read in my Bible today
That heaven is a beautiful place
I read in my Bible today,
It is filled with God's glory and
grace.
Walls of jasper, great and high
There no sin shall abide
Like transparent glass,
Streets of pure gold
Elegance   of   beauty   eyes
behold.
Twelve pearled gates,
Angels and tribes—

The children of Israel thereon
inscribed.
Twelve apostles name every
foundation-
They walk with those saved of
the nations,
Clear as crystal, a pure river
flows
The river of life, where the tree
of life grows-
From the throne of God and the
Lamb's creation,
The leaves of tree shall heal the
nation.
He shall wipe away all tears,
No more crying, --No pain--No
sorrows

Joy and peace   claim all our
tomorrows.

Chorus:
Keep your sights on the savior
Make your walk heaven bound,
Behold he comes quickly,
No cross, no crown.
Why not try Jesus,
Break the yoke of sin
He's Alpha and Omega,
The beginning and the end

A Family Affair

One day I asked, "Where's the
dentist?"
They told me, "on the Third
Street without a doubt".
So I traveled that road,
Up and down, to and fro
And round about,
Looking for a sign, ...some
indication,
When I noticed rows of houses
In a planned formation.
There I checked at every corner
And scanned every door
For the name plate that would
read.

Dentist MiMoore.
Finally, I found a little sign,
Hiding behind a young
palmetto tree.
"Eureka!", I yelled in high
falsetto.
In this town called Estill,
Hovers an unmistakable aire.
No outsiders, no intruders,
We are a family affair.

Southern Sympathy

Respect for funeral processions
in the big cities are lost,
People move in and out of those
dark Caravan processions just
to make better time on the
highway.
Some fall just short of beeping
The procession out of the way
In the presence of this solemn
ceremonial tradition people move
about as though they don't want
to be reminded about death.

What happened to those good
old days when people felt or at
least showed a pang of
sympathy upon recognizing
demise of his fellow human being,
by a visible show of respect. ---It
would seem until death hits home,
Our feelings are dead
concerning others.
Funeral processions seem to be
getting smaller and smaller,
Not so in South Carolina, I
soon discovered,------

One day while driving highway 601 North toward Hampton I noticed (*a good distance ahead*) cars and trucks
pulling over to the side of the road. For the life of me, I couldn't figure out what was going on. I looked down the highway for some sign of trouble,
I didn't see a fire truck, or an ambulance, or police cars flashing lights, But I did see a slow caravan of executive type cars moving toward me.

Is it the President of the USA?!?!!

Finally, I realized it was a funeral procession.

Whenever you pass by a church in South Carolina,

if the number of cars around the church appear as though the President of these United States of America is there,

You can rest assured it's a funeral.

The AIDS Commission

The march of death has begun,
The monster conceived,
Victory assured.
The unsuspecting victims
receive it with open arms.
Seeds of impending disaster
implanted,
Subtlety, slowly growing,
attacking the sheltered cells
unnoticed,

Except for the fierce but losing
battle

Staged by the inherent
resistance within..

When the carrier
acknowledges its presence..

This strange virus is usually
in full control,

Free will, in full bloom,
families are destroyed-

Tears flow heavily through
the homosexuals to the
heterosexuals,

Every community felt the
sting of death in its wake,
I often entertain the thought
that diseases reincarnate.
One disease replacing the
other.
Seemingly without end,
So long as the difference
between right and wrong
remains the resisted issue in
this society.
There is no final cure for this
plague,
Or the multitude to follow.

84

Aids is a curse, spread primarily through adherence to promiscuous appetites and illicit sex, blood transfusion, shooting needle. Until sin is arrested and given the eternal death sentence, or until we obey God's commands,

Our disobedience is Aids strongest ally.

Therefore, we the people, the Aids Commission.

~~~~~~~~~~~~~~~~~~~~~~~~~

Retirement

Today I would
go fishing,
But Tom wants me to take him
to Beaufort.
Yesterday Angela needed me
to be with her child at school.
Wednesday morning I was
relaxing on the porch, Jim's car
broke down-- He needed my
help. Thursday I took care of
some of my business,
A call was waiting my arrival back
home. Mrs. Jones needed some
wood cut,

She had burned her last piece.
Early Friday morning, my brother needed a ride to Charleston, SC, 90 miles away.
Saturday, a friend called and said their lights were about to be cut off,
That cost us $250.00.
Sunday I'm going to church,
But Monday, I'm looking for a job.

_____

A Valued Tradition
(an observation)

Speaking of tradition... some say are hard *(if ever)* to break.

For this tradition, I love grand ole South Carolina. Who, *(in my opinion)* is head and shoulders above anywhere I've ever traveled.

For the most part in the south houses are refurbished and built new to house our senior citizens when folks get old and sickly, they stay where they are loved the most, ...*at home with their families*. For the most part it is not poor economics. Its tradition... but most of all love.

The Land I Love
South Carolina
(early spring)

Flowers peek out here and
there, soon to appear in their
classic regalia.
Trees stand tall, strikingly
graceful against the heavens,
Innately   endowed   with
flourishing   green   leaves   and
pungent piney.
Trees of lesser appeal are
enriched with a beauty only God
can define.
The deciduous and evergreen

trees border most properties forming huge courtyards.

The lower lands maintain vivid wetness.   These areas constantly covered with water become the trees grave yard.

Man made ditches skirt the long winding lonely roads, careful not to mar its artistic view.... As it dips and climbs throughout this historic region in a snake like fashion.

Watch the wheat crop in the early spring during its infancy.

It stretches across the fields like a green grass skirt,
Proudly waving in the gentle crisp wind. There is something about the aborigines soil that soothes the mind when one is mesmerized by the sounds and sights of early spring.

Mile after mile of cultivated land... God and human designed landscape delight the senses, while absorbing the wonder of its imposing expanse and preserved beauty.

Only after the seed is planted
and pregnancy assured- shall we
witness her bountiful blessings -
The fruits of her labor.
There simmers a longing within
my being that transcends every
fiber of my thoughts -- to an
overwhelming need,
An acute realization of an
inherent   dependency...   an
instinctive desire to take care of
her. Knowing my need for it is
greater than its need for me.
During   this   moment   of
cogitation, my body and soul are
communing,

both keenly aware of the difference in the purpose of each others' existence.

Void of conscious thought, my hand and reaches downward to caress the earth and contain the loose soil in my grasp.
Emulating the child who clutches its mother's bosom,
Seeking to satisfy some of my many needs; I allow the earth to escape between my fingers like the sands in the hour glass—
Spilling away the time.

As I trudge with naked feet through the dislodged ground. I can feel her nurturing power tug gently at my roots.

The Play Daddy

I once knew a man named
Quilden
Who had fifteen children.
His first woman had five,
He left her for Ms. Sharon
McClive.
His second woman, who had
four, he gave her some money..
She needed more.
He got another job, to satisfy
her need,
He soon left her for Ms.
Carolyn Reed.

His fourth woman was to be his last,

He became concerned about his past.

When he had twelve, his number now even,

He soon left her for Ms. Janice Steven.

His rambling days are over now,

To this he did agree,

He finally married his sixth woman and fathered only three.

Time caught up to him honey!

The state DFS without fail,

Collects the due money

That keeps him out of jail.***

Signs of the Times
(school daze)

Up in the morning..

Drive to the school.

Retired, still earning my pay.

While our misguided youth

Have nothing to do

But run in the school hall and play.

Good Lord above, can't you hear we're crying,

Respect, its all but lost;

Please bring back those good old days,

When teachers prayed, and
counted the cost.
Bring back the prayer,
Bring back the paddle;
And there wasn't crack or
cocaine
To bring sorrow and shame to
your name.
The guns, the knives, the
fighting, the killing... when will it
all end!??
Who killed my brother,
Who killed my sisters,
Who killed my next of kin!???
Taken to jail, taken to trial,
Then back to jail again.

The signs of the times are upon our sin,
Lord, you sit high, you look low within,
You see all the trials we face,
Please grant us your saving grace.***

The End

www.ingramcontent.com/pod-product-compliance
Lightning Source LLC
Chambersburg PA
CBHW070815050426
42452CB00011B/2054